To My Friend

Jessica Lynn Slowikowski

With Love from

Julianna Rose Goblick

Date

July 15, 1998

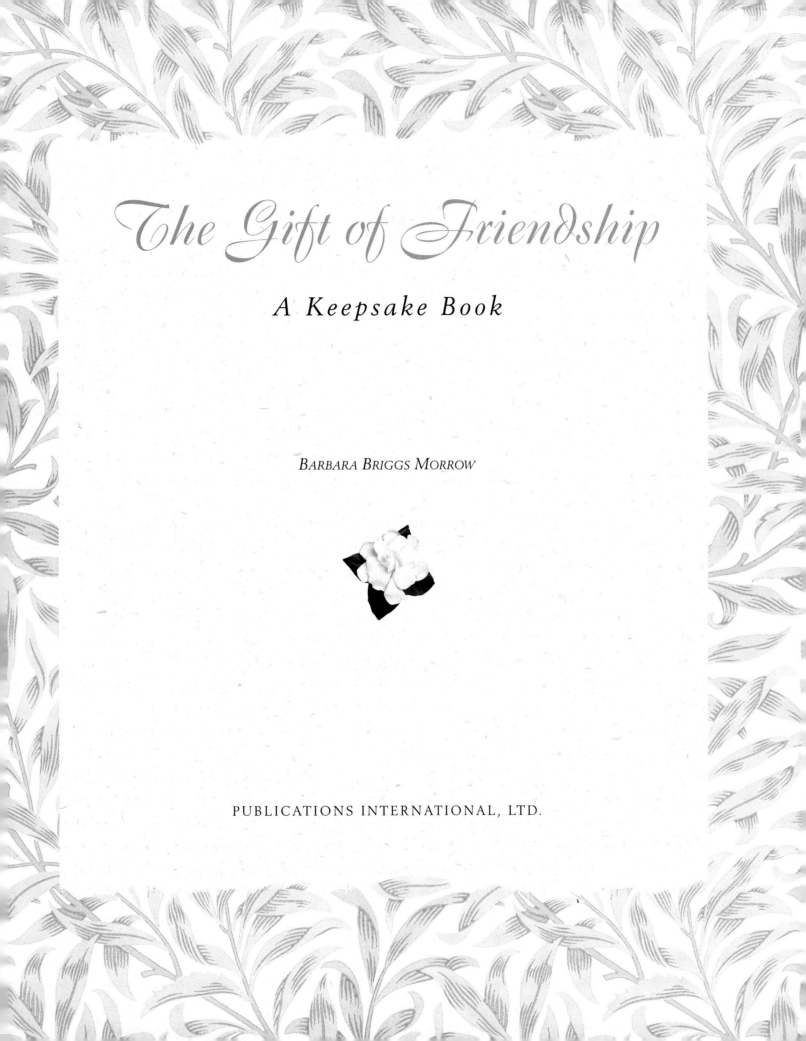

The Gift of Friendship

A Keepsake Book

BARBARA BRIGGS MORROW

PUBLICATIONS INTERNATIONAL, LTD.

Barbara Briggs Morrow is a contributing editor for *Midwest Living* magazine and a veteran writer whose work has appeared in *Cosmopolitan, Christian Science Monitor,* and the *Des Moines Register.* Her previous books include *American Country Sampler.*

Picture credits:
Jon Bradley/Tony Stone Images: 19; **Comstock:** 37, 44; **FPG International:** Ed Braverman: 49; Ron Chapble: 68; Rob Gage: 6; Rob Goldmen: 54; Michael Krasowitz: 14, 39; Richard Laird: 18; Rob Lang: 32; Ralph Mercer: 9; Michael Nelson: 4; Stephanie Rausser: 28; Ken Ross: 22; Mark Scott: 58; Telegraph Colour Library: 23, 25, 34, 40, 46; Arthur Tilley: 51; Jim Whitmes: 10; **Judah S. Harris:** 52, 66; **Images ©1996 PhotoDisc, Inc.:** 45, 55, 65; **International Stock:** Scott Barrow: 61; Vincent Graziani: 72; Michael Manheim: 64; John Michael: 33; **Frank Marchese:** 30; **Tom McCarthy/Rainbow:** 63; 16; **Planet Art:** Front cover border and interior border; **Rae Russell:** 42; **SuperStock:** 8, 17, 48, 62; **Transcendental Graphics:** 60.

Cover photo: **Kathleen Francour.**

Additional photography by **Brian Warling.**

Photo Stylist: **Sally Grimes.**

Photo Tinting Artist (interior photos): **Cheryl Winser.**

Flower consultation by Maria Vastis of Maria's Flower Boutique, Lincolnwood, IL
Flowers provided by Maria's Flower Boutique and Platz Wholesale Florist, Morton Grove, IL

CONTENTS

CHILDHOOD MEMORIES

Best Pals

Erin and Elizabeth lived next door to each other. Their bond formed instantly and grew stronger without encouragement from their busy parents. By the time their mothers noticed, the little girls were inseparable. They played dolls, and hide and seek, and fort, and restaurant, concocting gourmet entrees in the sandbox. They paused only for meals. Often they begged outdoor picnics from their mothers or insisted that the other one be invited over for dinner. At dusk, they chased fireflies while their mothers shook their heads in wonder that their joy in each other never seemed to wear out. The parents feared the friendship would falter after Erin's family moved, but whenever Erin and Elizabeth get together, they're best friends again.

"The song from beginning to end, I found again in the heart of a friend."

—Henry Wadsworth Longfellow, American poet

MY FIRST BEST FRIEND WAS _____.

WE PLAYED _____ FOR HOURS ON END.

WHEN WE HAD LUNCH TOGETHER, I HAD _____.

SHE LOVED TO EAT _____.

OUR FAVORITE TREAT WAS _____.

SHE THOUGHT _____ WAS ICKY.

I ALWAYS ADMIRED HER _____.

OUR BEST SECRET WAS _____.

SHE WAS AFRAID OF _____.

WE BOTH LOVED _____ (MOVIE, TV SHOW).

SHE PRETENDED TO BE _____.

I PRETENDED TO BE _____.

Grade School Days

We moved into the new house just in time for school to start. A girl whom I had seen at school always surrounded by friends lived down our new street. On the way to school one day I saw her walking just ahead of me so I shyly dawdled. She noticed me trailing behind and waited. I waved lamely and caught up. Before I could say a word, she was talking: "Hi! I'm Shelly. I've seen you at school. Your family is the one that just moved in." It was more of a statement than a question, but there was no time to answer. "We'll be friends. We'll walk to school together everyday." I didn't have to worry about what to say to her, because I hardly had a chance to do more than nod and smile. At first, I wondered what I had done to deserve this instant devotion. Then, I learned to simply enjoy it. Bubbly, determined Shelly had already decided we would be friends, and we were from that moment on.

"Little friends may prove great friends."

—Aesop, ancient Greek author

THE ELEMENTARY SCHOOL FRIEND I REMEMBER MOST OF ALL: _____.

AT RECESS, WE PLAYED _____.

AFTER SCHOOL, WE LOVED TO _____.

MY FAVORITE SUBJECT WAS _____.

_____ ALWAYS MADE US GIGGLE.

_____ WAS OUR FAVORITE TEACHER.

_____ WAS THE TEACHER WE LIKED LEAST OF ALL.

MY FRIENDS AND I LIKED JUST ABOUT ALL THE SAME THINGS:

BEST-LOVED BOOK(S):_____.

FAVORITE TV PROGRAM(S):_____.

SONG(S) WE SANG:_____.

AFTER-SCHOOL SNACKS:_____.

On My Block

For a child, a block, a street, or an apartment complex can form a whole world. The people who live there become friends and more—almost another family. What would the day be without a greeting from the lady in spike heels who walks her French poodle? Or, a little chat with the milkman? The children listen for the gentle whirl of the push mower belonging to the man next door. Grass neatly clipped, he tosses a ball around with any nearby kids, or he flags down the ice cream truck and springs for drippy bomb pops. In winter comes a running snowball war with the bunch from the next street. Both sides are hampered by the rag tag nature of their troops— from toddlers too bundled to move to teenage sisters too vain to wear hats and apt to quit because of near-frozen ears.

MEMORABLE NEIGHBORS: _____

_____.

MY YOUNGER FRIENDS WERE _____.

_____ WAS OLDER, BUT WE PLAYED TOGETHER.

WE WERE IN HOT WATER THE TIME THAT _____.

IN THE SUMMER, WE ALL LOVED TO _____.

WHEN WINTER CAME, WE _____.

A FAVORITE TREAT IN OUR NEIGHBORHOOD WAS _____.

"*Reinforce the stitch that ties us and I will do the same for you.*"

—Doris Scherwin, author

Just My Imagination

"Where's T'mongi's place?" my sister Lisa demanded as the family sat down to dinner. Nothing would comfort her until we set an extra place for this unseen guest. T'mongi, she informed us, came from an island, somewhere like Hawaii. She had beautiful, long, red hair and a grass skirt that swished when she moved. She was on vacation from her home and was staying in our china cabinet. Snickers turned to rapt attention as we imagined this exotic visitor. We were caught between envy and scorn because only Lisa seemed able to see her. Lisa continued to insist on the extra place and regaled us almost nightly with T'mongi's adventures and opinions. One evening, Lisa failed to set the extra place. When my father asked where her friend was, Lisa looked puzzled. Pressed, she told us T'mongi had gone home. Lisa didn't seem to mind, but the rest of us sorely missed our invisible guest.

"There she sits, a trifle loppy and loose-jointed, looking me squarely in the face in a straightforward, honest manner, a twinkle where her shoe-button eyes reflect the light . . . No wonder rag dolls are the best loved! You are so kindly, so patient, so lovable . . . ."

—The Original Adventures of Raggedy Ann *by Johnny Gruelle*

MY IMAGINARY FRIEND WAS _____.

I ALWAYS DESCRIBED HIM/HER AS _____.

I PRETENDED THAT WE _____.

AMONG THE STUFFED ANIMALS I HAD WERE _____

_____.

MY TOY _____ AND I WERE INSEPARABLE.

_____ GAVE ME MY FAVORITE TOY.

WE WERE TOGETHER CONSTANTLY UNTIL _____.

MY PARENTS THOUGHT THIS ATTACHMENT WAS _____.

OF MY CHILDHOOD TOYS, I STILL HAVE _____.

Keeping In Touch

Many members of the eighth-grade class hadn't seen each other since graduation day more than 20 years before. A number grumbled at the idea of getting together. Maybe they wouldn't recognize each other. After all, they were just children back then. Of course, everyone would have changed so much, gone in so many different directions. Laura didn't want to go. What if she didn't know anyone and no one knew her? But, the class president and chief organizer persisted. At the reunion, Laura studied women scattered in small groups across the old gym trying to glimpse the girls she had known. Then, a woman looked hard at her and smiled. "Laura?" she gasped. "It's Bonnie!" But, Laura had already recognized her friend, "Your smile is just the same." "Yours is, too," Bonnie answered.

PLACE PHOTOS OF
SCHOOL FRIENDS IN
THESE BLANK BOXES

GRADE SCHOOL FRIENDS WITH WHOM I'VE STAYED IN TOUCH: _____

_____ .

I WOULD LOVE TO SEE _____ *AGAIN.*

MEMORIES OF OUR LAST REUNION:

   LOCATION: _____ .

   ROLL CALL: _____

_____ .

WE ALL LAUGHED WHEN _____ *SURPRISED ME,*

BECAUSE _____ .

SOME IDEAS FOR OUR NEXT GET-TOGETHER:

_____

_____

_____

_____

YEARBOOK PORTRAITS

Best Friends

Best friends don't have to put into words what they mean to each other and what they expect from their relationship. They know on some unspoken level that "best" is shorthand for everything from listening when one of you needs to talk to lending out your favorite sweaters, even the new expensive one. You look forward to seeing each other, even if it's only been a little while since you parted. You can talk for hours or share a comfortable silence. You laugh at the same jokes, but you don't mind telling each other when you don't think something is the least bit funny. Countless small things— all of them unique and precious—make you "best" friends.

_____ WAS MY BEST HIGH SCHOOL FRIEND.

HER FAVORITES:

   COLOR: _____

   CLASSES: _____

   CLOTHES: _____

   SONG: _____

I ADMIRED HER _____.

WE RUSHED HOME TO WATCH _____ *ON* *TV.*

_____ *MADE HER CRY.*

_____ *WAS MY BEST COLLEGE FRIEND.*

WE MET WHEN _____.

OUR BIGGEST ADVENTURE WAS _____

_____.

AT LEAST ONCE A WEEK, SHE WORE _____.

THE ALBUM MOST LIKELY TO BE ON HER TURNTABLE WAS: _____.

Celebrations

After two days of trying to pick a day for a surprise birthday party for an unsuspecting friend, the phone threatens to attach permanently to Katie's ear, and her calendar is a mess of scribbled possibilities. Just when she thinks she has found a date that works for everyone, someone else calls. "I can't make it then," the caller says, "but what about...."
And Katie starts over, dialing to check yet another date with the rest of the group.
She and a half-dozen friends have been close for years. The friend they are planning the party for won't mind if there are no balloons, funny presents, or a cake from their favorite bakery. But, EVERYONE has to be there.

"A friend is a present you give yourself."

—Robert Louis Stevenson, Scottish novelist

MEMORABLE CELEBRATIONS

MOST MEMORABLE BIRTHDAY SPENT WITH FRIENDS: _____

_____.

I REMEMBER IT SO WELL, BECAUSE _____

_____.

OF ALL THE GIFTS RECEIVED FROM FRIENDS, I CHERISH _____.

BEST PARTY I HELPED PLAN FOR A FRIEND: _____

_____.

IT WOULDN'T HAVE BEEN A PARTY UNLESS WE SERVED _____.

MOST MEMORABLE NON-BIRTHDAY CELEBRATION: _____

_____.

_____ GAVE THE BEST PARTIES, REGARDLESS OF THE OCCASION.

Graduation Memories

On graduation day, my friend _____ said something I'll always

remember: _____

_____ .

During graduation, I stood next to _____

and _____ while waiting to get my diploma.

_____ was our class valedictorian.

_____ threw the best graduation party of all.

We danced to _____ .

As usual, _____ stole the show on the dance floor.

For graduation, my parents gave me _____ .

My most cherished keepsake from graduation is _____ .

Other graduation goodies: _____

_____ .

Memorable Nights

$\mathcal{P}$illars that supported the cafeteria ceiling turned into spreading maples with brown construction-paper bark and green crepe-paper foliage. The usual folding tables sported checkered cloths like those in magazine pictures of outdoor cafes. Patches of grass carefully fringed with borrowed sewing scissors covered parts of the dingy linoleum. We marveled as we watched "Barefoot in the Park" take shape, congratulating ourselves and each other on choosing the perfect theme for the prom. Standing together surveying our creation, we could almost see sunshine filtering through our hand-crafted canopy of branches and feel soft spring breezes stirring the grass. We all agreed the room looked just like a park—even better. Our decorations worked magic, we thought. None of us realized that on that magic night, and on many others, it was our friendship that cast the spell.

MY PROM DATE WAS _____.

HE WORE _____ AND I WORE _____.

AT THE PROM, I ALSO DANCED WITH _____

_____.

OUR PROM THEME WAS _____.

"Do you love me

Now that I can dance?

WATCH ME NOW!"

—*"Do You Love Me" recorded by The Contours, 1962*

BEST REMEMBERED DANCES AND DATES

DANCE: _____ MY DATE WAS _____.

DANCE: _____ MY DATE WAS _____.

DANCE: _____ MY DATE WAS _____.

_____ WAS GUARANTEED TO GET

MY FRIENDS OUT ONTO THE DANCE FLOOR.

MY FRIEND _____ AND I DOUBLE-DATED WITH _____

AND _____ TO GO TO _____.

MY FRIEND _____ WAS THE BEST DANCER.

Important Firsts

During these years, we face one beginning after another—exciting, nerve-wracking, happy, slightly scary beginnings. We depend on true friends to help us through these firsts, whether it's a gear-crunching initial bout with a stick shift or hours of trying on outfits and wringing our hands before a first date.

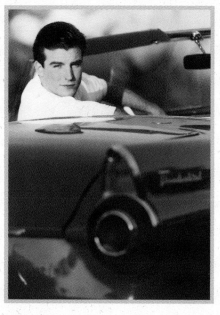

WHEN *I* WENT OUT ON MY FIRST DATE WITH

_____,

I TALKED OVER ALL THE PARTICULARS WITH

_____.

HER ADVICE: _____

_____.

AS SOON AS *I* GOT MY DRIVER'S LICENSE,

_____ AND *I* WENT CRUISING.

SHE WAS GREAT ABOUT REMINDING ME TO: _____.

WHEN _____ GAVE ME MY FIRST KISS,

I COULDN'T WAIT TO TELL _____.

SHE SAID: _____.

ON OUR FIRST SOLO TRIP, _____ AND *I* TRAVELED TO _____.

Just Friends

Of course, "just" never describes any friend. Male friends play important roles, too.
Besides sharing good times, they give advice from a perspective you'll never have
and can stand in for a date when you need one.

My closest male friend was _____.

He was famous for his _____.

What I admired most about him was _____.

The best advice he ever gave me: _____

_____.

His favorite pastime was _____.

After he graduated from high school/college, he _____

_____.

When he raided the refrigerator, he would grab _____.

"Well, the winter's gone, and I've written no books, earned no fortune; but I've made a friend worth having and I'll try to keep him all my life."

—*Jo March in* Little Women *by novelist Louisa May Alcott*

Footsteps To Follow

As high school freshmen, we were, we thought, very grown-up, much too old to be read to and especially too old for a book like *Charlotte's Web*. But, our teacher insisted and, even though most of us were taller than she, no one would have dared argue. Though she was barely five feet tall in sensible pumps, with reading glasses perched at the end of her nose and a trademark scarf tied jauntily at her neck, her most soft-spoken request held the force of law. Maybe that was because conviction shone in her eyes. You could see she KNEW she was right—especially about this book. In spite of ourselves, we listened rapt as she read the story of Charlotte the spider and her growing friendship with Wilbur the pig. Doing voices for the characters and pronouncing each sentence with infinite care, she told the story so effectively that the class begged her to continue when our daily story time ended. By the bittersweet conclusion, we were not only enthralled with the story but also with language itself.

PLACE PHOTO OF SOMEONE YOU ADMIRE HERE

"Wilbur never forgot Charlotte. Although he loved her children and grandchildren dearly, none of the new spiders ever quite took her place in his heart."

—Charlotte's Web *by children's author E.B. White*

I LOOKED UP TO _____.

SHE WAS MY _____.

OF ALL HER EXCEPTIONAL QUALITIES, I ADMIRED _____ MOST OF ALL.

IT MADE A LASTING IMPRESSION ON ME WHEN SHE SAID _____

_____.

WHEN I THINK OF HER, I THINK OF _____.

IF WE COULD TALK RIGHT NOW, I WOULD MOST LIKE TO TELL HER _____

_____.

SHE WOULD BE SURPRISED BY SOME OF THE TURNS MY LIFE HAS TAKEN, ESPECIALLY _____

_____.

I THINK SHE WOULD BE PROUD THAT I _____

_____.

27

Slumber Party Particulars

The sleepless crew: _____

_____ .

Snack attacks: _____ .

Truth or Dare you to list party pastimes: _____ .

We listened to _____ , *until the parents*

thought they would lose their minds.

Midnight Mischief: _____

_____ .

Now we can laugh at the time we _____ .

When cruisin' the hangouts, _____ *had wheels,* _____

rode shotgun, and _____ *came along for the ride.*

We headed straight for _____ .

We sang along to _____ *on the car radio.*

If I had a time machine, I would travel back to _____ .

My friends _____ *would be there.*

We would _____ .

Keeping in Touch

The changes that sweep through our lives at this stage scatter friends like fallen leaves in a gust of wind. Give a departing companion an address book filled with her friends' addresses, birthdays, and important dates already filled in. Update your address book from time to time and copy changes to share with friends. Keeping in touch takes more than good intentions. Maintaining long-distance friendships requires organization and perserverance. Making the effort can mean holding fast to friendships that otherwise might slip away.

DATES TO REMEMBER FOR KEEPING IN TOUCH WITH HIGH SCHOOL AND COLLEGE PALS:

_____

_____

_____

_____

_____

LETTER-WRITING TIME SEEMS TO GROW MORE SCARCE EVERY YEAR. SEND A CARD WITH A BRIEF HELLO AND A MEMENTO TUCKED INTO IT. OR SUBSTITUTE AN OLD SNAPSHOT OF THE TWO OF YOU, A PACKET OF FLOWER SEEDS, A CARTOON CLIPPED FROM THE NEWSPAPER, OR A COPY OF A FAVORITE RECIPE. USE THIS SPACE TO JOT DOWN OTHER KEEPING-IN-TOUCH TIPS.

_____

_____

_____

_____

_____

CHOSEN PATHWAYS

Best Friends

From career moves to new relationships, choices and beginnings threaten to overwhelm everyone at times. "What do you think I should do? I mean, really?," you ask almost rhetorically. Close friends know when to answer this question honestly and when your best interests require them to reserve judgement. The answer might not be the one you were hoping to hear, but a best friend will tell you anyway. She also knows when to pry you away from your moody thoughts to go to a movie, take a walk in the park, or treat you to a mountainous chocolate sundae.

> *"If we don't change, we don't grow. If we don't grow, we are not really living."*
>
> —Gail Sheehy, journalist and author

_____ AND I CLICKED IMMEDIATELY, AS IF WE HAD BEEN BEST

FRIENDS FOREVER.

SHE WAS THE ONE WHO CONVINCED ME TO _____

_____.

SHE WARNED ME NOT TO _____.

HER FAVORITE SPOT WAS _____.

SHE NEVER COULD RESIST _____.

WHENEVER SHE WANTED TO CHEER ME UP, SHE _____

_____.

SHE TALKED OFTEN ABOUT _____.

I VALUE HER _____ MOST OF ALL.

Working Relationships

We worked side by side at our first real jobs. Over slightly smooshed brown-bag lunches, we talked of the day when our potential would be recognized and we would be tapped for more responsible positions. She was promoted first, and I struggled to be happy for her. I decided I would no longer look for her at lunchtime. She would probably be busy getting to know her new co-workers. They'd probably go out to lunch. That first morning rushed past, as I hunched over a project. I had just decided to eat at my desk when I heard a paper sack scrunching impatiently behind me. "What are you doing? Aren't you eating today? Wait til you hear what they have me doing...."
After more months of brown-bag lunches, I was promoted, and better prepared for it, thanks to my friend's insight and experience.

When someone asked Abraham Lincoln, after he was elected president, what he was going to do about his enemies, he replied, "I'm going to destroy them. I am going to make them my friends."

—Attributed to Lincoln, unverified

ON-THE-JOB FRIENDS:

_____

_____

_____.

WE GET TOGETHER AT _____.

WHEN I'M STRESSED, MY BEST WORK FRIEND SAYS _____

_____.

AROUND THE OFFICE, SHE'S KNOWN AS _____.

IF _____ IS NEEDED, YOU CAN DEPEND ON HER.

IF I COULD BORROW JUST ONE OF HER SKILLS, I WOULD CHOOSE _____.

IF SHE WON THE LOTTERY, SHE WOULD _____

_____.

On Our Own

My dad thought my first car should be a formidable machine, something substantial enough to hold its own amid barreling tractor trailers, daydreaming Sunday drivers, and the other denizens of the open road. Buy one in the most unappealing color on the lot, he advised, you'll get a great deal—and, don't be suckered into paying for any frills such as a radio or bucket seats. That's why I took my best friend along to see the car I wanted to buy. It was small enough to fit inside Dad's automobile. Painted a shimmering pearlized blue with cute, white leather bucket seats, and a jaunty stick-shift, this car practically whispered my name. My friend loved it as much as I did and praised my excellent judgement, giving me the courage to make an offer. When I drove it to my parents' house, my father's reaction surprised me. "It's your car," he said. "You're the one who has to like it."

My first big purchase counseled by friends: _____.

My first car was a _____ *, and* _____ *was the first*

friend I took for a ride.

On-our-own trips together:

   Where: _____ *With whom:* _____.

   Where: _____ *With whom:* _____.

   Where: _____ *With whom:* _____.

My folks would have flipped if they knew about the time when _____

and I _____.

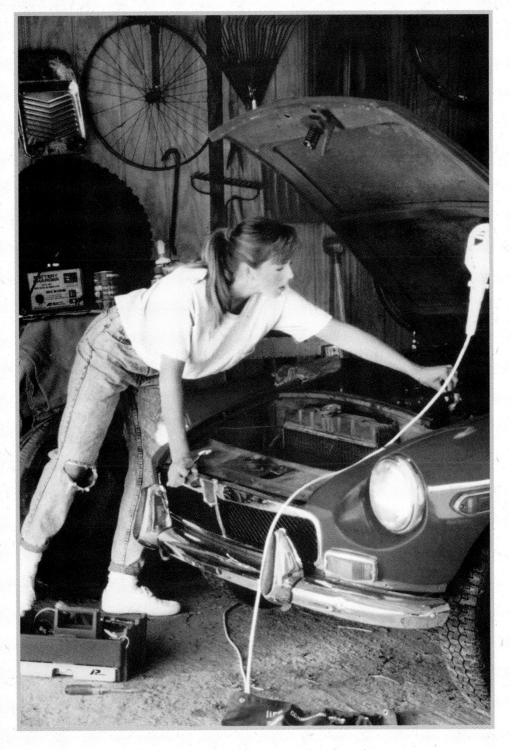

"*A woman is like a teabag. It's only when she's in
hot water that you realize how strong she is.*"

—*Nancy Reagan, address to U.S. Women's Congress, 1981*

Roommates Remembered

A relationship rises to a new level when friends share a bathroom sink and closet space. Surprise! That well-groomed person you like so much leaves toothpaste globs and a trail of dirty socks. The girl who never has anything to wear owns enough clothes to open a boutique; she insists on hanging all of them up and won't let you borrow any of them. But, you are always pleasantly surprised when she bakes you cookies to cheer you up and courteously lets you have the first shower when you're running late. If you weather the surprises—good and bad—cohabitating will bring you closer than ever.

_____ *AND I BECAME ALMOST LIKE SISTERS.*

HER HABIT THAT SURPRISED ME THE MOST: _____.

HABIT(S) THAT SHE TAUGHT ME: _____.

_____ *WAS TV NIGHT. THE DIAL WAS TURNED TO* _____.

SHE FAITHFULLY STOCKED THE KITCHEN WITH _____.

HER LEAST FAVORITE CHORES: _____.

I COULD COUNT ON HER TO _____

_____.

WHAT SHE WOULD SAY SHE MISSES MOST ABOUT OUR ROOMMATE DAYS: _____

_____.

"...the only way to have a friend is to be one."

—Ralph Waldo Emerson, American essayist and poet

Through Thick and Thin

"It might be for the best. You deserve better." You wish you could think of something more original to say. You're afraid those words and dozens of other expressions of support and comfort will sound hollow, even though you believe them sincerely and hope your troubled friend will, too. She looks across the table. Her pained expression eases for a moment. "Keep saying that," she says. "Coming from you, it helps."

_____ WAS THERE FOR ME WHEN _____

_____ .

IT HELPED MORE THAN SHE REALIZED WHEN SHE _____

_____ .

ADVICE FROM A FRIEND THAT I WILL PASS ALONG TO OTHERS IN NEED: _____

_____ .

How to be a Lifesaver

1. Take over a meal (carry-out will do, but make it something that can freeze for a day or two).

2. Don't just offer to stop by. Ask her to set up a specific time. Bring along a book, a game, a popular video, or another treat.

3. Gently bring up what's troubling her. She may be concerned that she's burdening you about it, so give her an opening to talk.

4. Offer to run errands, such as picking up the cleaning or stopping at the grocery store.

5. Coax her to go outdoors. A walk in the park, a visit to a botanical garden, or a stroll around the neighborhood will lift both your spirits.

Keeping in Touch

When we lived in the same city and our children were the same age, we talked almost every day. Our discussions rambled from the relative merits of disposable diaper brands to ground-breaking 19th-century novelists to recipes for making chicken taste more exciting. These days, separated by several states, we manage only a note or a phone call or two every year. I send off a card, jotting only a fraction of what I would like to tell her. Reluctantly, I follow up with a phone call. "Well, how ARE you?" she exclaims, but the voice is joyous and teasing without a trace of rebuke. Then, before I can say another word, she's apologizing for being out of touch, reciting a familiar litany of responsibilities and exhausted evenings. We're helpless victims of this frantic stage of life, we agree. Our friendship, rooted deeply in a quieter time, can thrive without much tending for awhile.

FRIENDS I STILL FEEL CLOSE TO EVEN THOUGH WE NOW LIVE FAR APART:

_____

_____

IF I HAD UNLIMITED TIME, I WOULD VISIT _____, *BECAUSE*

_____.

IF I MISS A BIRTHDAY OR OTHER OCCASION, _____ *WILL*

APPRECIATE HEARING FROM ME ON _____. *THAT DATE IS SPECIAL*

BECAUSE _____.

HAVING GIVEN UP ON GETTING CHRISTMAS CARDS OUT IN TIME, ONE WOMAN SENDS

HAPPY VALENTINE'S DAY GREETINGS. FRIENDS TAUGHT ME THESE LESS-THAN-ORTHODOX

IDEAS FOR KEEPING IN TOUCH:

_____

_____

_____

LIFE'S LANDMARKS

Best Friends

You're tempted to ignore birthdays, anniversaries, and other landmark dates as you get older. Fortunately, close friends hardly ever allow that. Maryann shows up with still-warm peach cobbler despite declarations that there would be no celebrating. Deborah thinks no one knows her birthday or age, until friends ring the doorbell at 9:00 A.M. and roust her out, rumpled and sleepy-eyed, for a birthday breakfast. Maribeth always sends her friends anniversary cards, a pleasant and welcome reminder of the value of friendship.

BIRTHDAY SURPRISES AND OTHER THOUGHTFUL GESTURES FROM MY FRIENDS:

_____

_____

FRIENDS' ANNIVERSARIES TO REMEMBER:

_____

_____

WHO CAN RESIST A BIRTHDAY LUNCH? FAVORITE RESTAURANTS OF MY FRIENDS:

_____ _____

_____ _____

_____ _____

FOR FUTURE REFERENCE—FAVORITE COLLECTIBLES, TREATS, AND BOOKS OF MY FRIENDS.

_____ _____

_____ _____

_____ _____

Love at First...

"I'm going to marry that man," I announced to my best friend as soon as I knew, long before I would have let him in on my intentions. He might have thought I was crazy at that point, considering our relationship was all of a month old. My friend of many years, however, knew me well enough to start shopping for a bridesmaid's dress.

FIRST FRIEND I TOLD THAT HE WAS THE ONE: _____.

HER REACTION: _____.

OF ALL MY FRIENDS, HE AND _____ GET ALONG

ESPECIALLY WELL. THEY ALWAYS TALK ABOUT _____.

MY FRIEND _____ TOLD ME FIRST WHEN SHE FELL IN LOVE. I SAID:

_____.

FIXING UP FRIENDS IS RISKY BUSINESS, BUT IN THIS CASE IT WORKED OUT:

_____

_____.

IN THIS CASE IT DIDN'T WORK OUT:

_____

_____.

Down the Aisle

For the bridesmaids, Michelle's mother had her heart set on wine-colored Empire waist floor-length dresses with flowing sleeves and yards of lace trim. We looked like a bevy of understudies for the part of Juliet in a none-to-promising Shakespeare revival. But, we all swore that we loved the gowns and were sure we would wear them again. When our turns came, Michelle did the same for us. A bridesmaid's most important job is being a good friend to the bride.

"...A good marriage is based on the talent for friendship."

—Human, All Too Human *by Friedrich Nietzsche, German philosopher*

REMEMBERING BRIDESMAIDS AND GROOMSMEN:

_____

_____

_____.

_____ ACTED ABOVE AND BEYOND THE CALL OF DUTY, WHEN

_____.

CHERISHED GIFTS FROM FRIENDS:

_____

_____.

FRIENDS' WEDDINGS I WAS PART OF:

_____

_____.

COUNT ON _____ FOR A MEMORABLE WEDDING TOAST.

FOR EXAMPLE: _____.

All in the Family

*I*f we're fortunate, beloved family members also become valued friends. Dozens of small events mark this passage: the first time you tease your mother out of a bad mood, when you realize you'd rather get together with your sister than anyone else, or when you call your sister-in-law just to chat. Loving each other comes naturally; liking each other strengthens that bond.

BESIDES BEING MY _____, _____ IS ONE

OF MY CLOSEST FRIENDS.

WE ENJOY MANY OF THE SAME THINGS, INCLUDING _____.

_____ IS A TRADITION IN OUR FAMILY.

WHEN OUR FAMILY GATHERS FOR A MEAL, EVERYONE LOOKS FORWARD TO _____

_____.

OUR FAMILY'S FAVORITE DISHES:

_____

_____

_____.

_____ MAKES EVERYONE LAUGH. PERENNIAL FAMILY JOKE:

_____

_____.

"...I want to go home to the hill country. That's the part of the world where people know when you're sick, miss you when you die...."

—*Samuel E. Johnson, speaking to his son Lyndon B. Johnson*

Baby Days

"Look! Look what he's doing!" My friend's shouts bring me running terror-stricken from the back of the house to the living room where she sits with my six-month-old son. "What's wrong?" I gasp, fearing concussions, household poisons, or worse. Everything looks normal. Jonathan is rocking back and forth on his knees, grinning happily. "Nothing, but I thought you should see this," my friend insists. I hated to tell her he had been doing this first-step-toward-crawling routine for a week. Her amazement makes me take a second look and appreciate my son for the little miracle he is.

"Children reinvent your world for you."

—Susan Sarandon, actress

WHEN I FOUND OUT I WAS PREGNANT, I COULDN'T WAIT TO TELL _____.

MY FRIEND _____ AND MY CHILD _____

SEEMED TO SHARE A BOND FROM THE BEGINNING.

_____ TAUGHT MY CHILD _____ HOW TO _____.

I TAUGHT MY FRIEND _____'S CHILD HOW TO _____.

_____ IS MY CHILDREN'S FAVORITE BABYSITTER.

_____ AND I BECAME FRIENDS BECAUSE OUR

CHILDREN PLAYED TOGETHER.

THE KIDS LOVED IT WHEN WE _____.

_____ WAS OUR FAVORITE TREAT.

A Couple of Friends

They pulled into our driveway unannounced on the way home from an errand. They are sure they'll be welcome, and they are. Sweaty from yard work and other Saturday chores, we rush out to meet them. "Come on. Stay for dinner," my husband says. I clear a spot at the kitchen table so we can sit down, not really caring about the clutter. We've known this couple since our college days, and we know they really won't mind if dinner's not fancy and the house isn't spotless. We like the same things; our kids are close in age; we make each other laugh and share similar worries. "Don't take this the wrong way," my friend says as we work together to pitch the paper plates after dinner, "but, it's nice to be somewhere where you don't feel like guests."

I know what she means; we feel just as comfortable at their house.

"When friends stop being frank and useful to each other,
the world loses some of its brilliance."

—Anatole Broyard, book reviewer and editor for The New York Times

COUPLES WE'RE CLOSE TO:

_____

_____.

HOW WE MET OUR CLOSEST PAIR OF FRIENDS: _____

_____.

THE FOUR OF US ENJOY _____

_____.

OUR FAVORITE RESTAURANT IS _____.

A FABULOUS WEEKEND OR VACATION WE SPENT TOGETHER WAS _____

_____.

WE LIKE A LOT OF THE SAME THINGS, BUT THERE ARE EXCEPTIONS. FOR INSTANCE

_____

_____.

Keeping in Touch

Watching friends' children grow up can be startling. While adults congratulate themselves on not changing much since they've known each other, children seem to transform before your eyes. Suddenly, the thumb-sucking, pigtailed toddler is a poised graduate. The whiney half-pint with the crew cut towers over you and politely shakes your hand. When you compliment their manners or ask about their progress, watch your friends' eyes light up. Taking an interest in each other's children and families can be one of the most rewarding ways to keep in touch.

PLACE PHOTOS
OF FRIENDS'
CHILDREN IN
PHOTO BOXES

BIRTHDAYS OF MY FRIENDS' CHILDREN:

_____

_____

_____

_____

FUTURE GRADUATIONS, COMMUNIONS, OR OTHER IMPORTANT EVENTS:

_____

_____

_____

SPECIAL INTERESTS OF MY FRIENDS' CHILDREN:

_____

_____

_____

_____

GRANDCHILDREN OF MY FRIENDS:

_____

_____

_____

Best Friends

Over coffee, Mary told Irene in no uncertain terms what she thought of her ideas for the annual club dinner. Irene argued back, dismissing Mary's opinion with a wave of her hand. Mary rose in disgust and stormed into the kitchen to check on dinner. When she returned, they turned merrily to other topics, though they had not resolved a thing. Irene's granddaughter was coloring nearby and stopped scribbling to stare. Finally, the little girl interrupted, "Why do you argue like that? I thought you were friends." The women laughed, and Mary explained, "Your grandma and I can say what we really think to each other because we are such good friends."

"I find friendship to be like wine, raw when new, ripened with age...."

—Thomas Jefferson, third president of the United States

LONG-STANDING FRIENDS: _____

_____

_____.

_____ AND I ARE CLOSE EVEN THOUGH

WE'VE KNOWN EACH OTHER FOR ONLY A SHORT TIME.

I CAN COUNT ON _____ TO _____.

SHE DEPENDS ON ME TO _____.

_____ HAS TAUGHT ME MUCH ABOUT BEING A GOOD FRIEND.

ONE LESSON STANDS OUT: _____

_____.

Fellow Travelers

*T*raveling together takes some of the worry and the tedium out of planning, waiting in airports, and navigating strange places. Best of all, you and your companion share discoveries and adventures—a quaint cafe, a breathtaking view, an innkeeper's warm welcome. You may also share disasters—lost tickets, run-down motels, monsoons in the dry season—which are less catastrophic because you face them together. From double sets of snapshots to insights you would have missed on your own, the memories are richer.

MY FAVORITE TRAVELING COMPANIONS: _____

_____ .

OUR BEST TRIP TOGETHER: _____ .

SHE PREFERRED THE TRIP TO _____ .

THE MOST BEAUTIFUL PLACE WE VISITED WAS _____ .

THE BIGGEST TRAVEL CHALLENGE WE FACED: _____

_____ .

OUR TRAVEL WISH LIST OF PLACES WE WANT TO GO: _____

_____

_____ .

"Sometimes, with luck, we find the kind of true friend, male or female, that
appears only two or three times in a lucky lifetime, one that will winter us
and summer us, grieve, rejoice, and travel with us."

—Barbara Holland, *poet*

61

Animal Friends

There's one friend who's always glad to see me. Stella, a large, black and tan canine of uncertain lineage, is never cross, never needs cheering up, and is always glad to do what I suggest—with the exceptions of a bath with flea soap or a trip to that sneaky veterinarian. When I first got Stella from the local shelter, I took her to the vet and asked about her probable parentage. The vet shook her head and refused to guess, "Too much dog in there to tell." All Stella asks for is a pat once in a while and a kind word or two. At times, I can't help feeling unworthy of this unfailing devotion.

FIRST PET: _____.

LONGEST-STANDING ANIMAL FRIEND: _____

_____.

_____ WAS A TRUE WATCH

_____. OF ALL MY PETS,

_____ DESERVES THE PERSONALITY AWARD.

SOME OF HER/HIS ANTICS: _____

_____.

FAVORITE PET TREATS: _____.

MY MOST UNUSUAL PET: _____.

MY FRIEND _____'S PET AND I HAVE A _____

RELATIONSHIP. SHE/HE ALWAYS GREETS ME WITH _____.

*"Animals are such agreeable friends—they ask
no questions, they pass no criticisms."*

—George Eliot, English novelist

Wit and Wisdom

Liz has been making us all laugh for as long as we can remember. But, when I look back on her funny stories I can't think of a single one that's not about her and her shortcomings. She tells tales of a family that never eats anywhere but in her car and of an extra room so cluttered that she once lost a bag of Christmas presents until March. She reports that her husband is threatening to keep socks in their safety deposit box so he will know where to find at least one clean, matching pair. Liz never mentions the college course she teaches, how bright her children are, or the fact that her husband's face lights up when she walks into a room. We're all too busy laughing to mention it ourselves. Her friends giggle until mascara-heavy tears streak down our faces, and we all feel better about our own lives. She would dismiss this as a small thing, but to her friends it's a great gift. Of course, every time I try to tell her, we both end up laughing.

"I think laughter may be a form of courage. . . . As humans, we sometimes stand tall and look into the sun and laugh. And I think we are never more brave than when we do that."

—Linda Ellerbee, journalist

I APPRECIATE _____'S SENSE OF HUMOR.

I'LL NEVER FORGET THE STORY ABOUT _____

_____.

_____ MAKES HER SO SPECIAL.

SHE LOVES _____.

SHE HATES _____.

WHEN I'M TROUBLED, I TALK TO _____.

HER WISEST ADVICE: _____

_____.

_____ COMES TO ME FOR HELP.

OFTEN, I HAVE TOLD HER _____

_____.

Never Say Goodbye

Separated by half of the country, my friend and I plan a visit. We had pledged to get together regularly, but somehow 20 years have passed since the last time we saw each other. It couldn't be that long, we both said at first. Yes, unbelievably, 20 years had gone, but where? Driving to her house, I feared the afternoon would be awkward. So much had happened. Surely we both had changed beyond catching up. But, as I stepped out of the car, she flew out the door and flung her arms around me. I knew then that nothing that really mattered had changed between us.

"There are three things that grow more precious with age: old wood to burn,
old books to read, and old friends to enjoy."

—*Vern McLellan, author*

EVEN THOUGH WE LIVE FAR APART, I'VE STAYED CLOSE TO _____.

MAINTAINING A LONG-DISTANCE FRIENDSHIP CAN BE DIFFICULT. WE STAY IN TOUCH BY

_____.

A FEW OF HER FAVORITE THINGS:

COLOR _____

FRAGRANCE _____

FLOWERS _____

HOBBIES _____

AUTHORS _____

OUR DREAM GET-TOGETHER: _____

BIRTHDAYS AND OTHER IMPORTANT DATES OF MY OTHER FAR-AWAY FRIENDS:

_____

_____

_____

_____.

Applause, Applause

No chips and bottled salsa when you visit Amy's house. Half the fun is guessing what luscious creation will greet your arrival—maybe a flan topped with exquisitely sauced fresh berries or a delicately coated brie surrounded by baked-from-scratch flat breads. Amy, pretty and unruffled, glides into the room with her latest culinary work of art as if it had appeared magically in the kitchen. Check the kitchen and you might wonder if that were indeed the case. The countertops sparkle, and there's no hint of cooking clutter. Friends react to Amy's talent with the sort of awe reserved for prima ballerinas and Olympic athletes. She makes gourmet cooking look easy, but we know it isn't. We don't dare ask for recipes anymore than we would try to duplicate an Olympic gymnast's routine. We just praise the results.

I ADMIRE _____'S GIFT FOR _____.

HOW SHE CAME BY HER SKILL: _____

_____.

HOW MY FRIENDS SHARE THEIR TALENTS: _____

_____.

_____ IS ONE OF THE MOST TALENTED COOKS I KNOW.

OF HER CREATIONS, MY FAVORITE IS _____.

HER RECIPE: _____

_____

_____

_____

_____

_____

I Knew Her When

I know a different side of Mary Ann than almost anyone else. At first glance, I see what everyone sees—a stylish, successful woman who has risen through the ranks to become a vice president in a large corporation. Then, her easy smile and gentle drawl take me back to our college days. Then, she was a sweet girl from a poor family living in a tiny Southern town. Teachers told her she wasn't college material, but she was confident that hard work would make up for any shortcomings. She fought her way to a 4.0 average with countless all-nighters and endless tutoring sessions. Despite her grueling schedule, Mary Ann found time to make chicken and creamy white gravy for her homesick roommates. She never seemed to have any problems—only challenges and goals. That still describes Mary Ann, and she still makes time for her friends.

Place photo of a
friend here

"When the leaves of this autograph are yellow with age, and when the lines I write here on this page fade, please remember me kindly and do not forget all that we send into the lives of others comes back into our own."

—*Inscription in a child's school autograph book, author unknown, c. 1930s*

MY FRIEND _____ WENT ON TO BIG THINGS,

INCLUDING _____.

OTHERS WOULD BE SURPRISED TO KNOW THAT SHE _____

_____.

WHEN WE TALKED ABOUT THE FUTURE, SHE ALWAYS SAID _____

_____.

WE GOT ALONG BECAUSE _____.

IN HER YEARBOOK, SHE WOULD HAVE BEEN IDENTIFIED AS THE PERSON MOST LIKELY TO

_____.

HOW WE STAY IN TOUCH: _____

_____.

Keeping in Touch

A couple of years ago, the boxes of snapshots that needed to be arranged into albums threatened to take over the basement storage area. Forget the scrapbooks—shoe boxes with index cards marking dates and occasions would have to do. I filed some favorite photos of friends and the times we spent together; others I stowed in envelopes marked with their names. These pictures, along with a shot or two of me and my family and others we care about, went into friendship albums that became Christmas gifts. My friends—all too busy for scrapbooks as well—said it was the best present they received.

IF I MADE A PHOTO SCRAPBOOK, THESE FRIENDS' PHOTOS WOULD BE INCLUDED WITH CAPTIONS THAT READ:

_____ CAPTION: _____.

_____ CAPTION: _____.

_____ CAPTION: _____.

_____ CAPTION: _____.

THESE FRIENDS HAVE A TALENT FOR KEEPING IN TOUCH. THEIR TIPS:

_____ TIP: _____.

_____ TIP: _____.

_____ TIP: _____.

REUNION NOTES. LIST IMPORTANT UPCOMING DATES AND FRIENDS TO CONTACT:

_____ CONTACT: _____.

_____ CONTACT: _____.

_____ CONTACT: _____.